The Empowering Process

*Daily Mindful Questions to Add Value, Gain Clarity,
and Increase Results in Your Life Right Now*

Gail Kraft

Crystal Pointe Media, Inc.
San Diego, CA

The Empowering Process

Daily Mindful Questions to Add Value, Gain Clarity, and Increase Results in Your Life Right Now

Gail Kraft

Copyright 2016
Published by Crystal Pointe Media, Inc.
San Diego, California

ISBN-13: 978-1539917519

ISBN-10: 1539917517

gail@theempoweringprocess.com

DISCLAIMER

The contents of this publication are intended for educational and informative use only. They are not to be considered directive nor as a guide to self-diagnosis or self-treatment. Before embarking on any therapeutic regimen, it is absolutely essential that you consult with and obtain the approval of your personal physician or health care provider.

Cover & Interior Design by Victoria Vinton

"I believe that imagination is stronger than knowledge. That myth is more potent than history. That dreams are more powerful than facts. That hope always triumphs over experience. That laughter is the only cure for grief. And I believe that love is stronger than death."

ROBERT FULGHUM

Acknowledgements

This book has been completed with the support and love of my family, David and Charlotte Kraft, David and Katie Cerra, and Kerri Pacheco. It was first inspired as declarations due to Reignite by New Peaks and later refined to empowering questions for impact and clarity due to Supreme Influence In Action (SIIA) by Niurka, Inc.

The Reignite and SIIA community have supported and encouraged me along the way and have been a great inspiration to these pages. My clients have shared their struggles, which has resulted in many of these questions being written for them specifically. Stephanie Burns from Chic CEO was an amazing mentor and supporter, keeping me focused and on track. I thank you all so much for inspiring this work.

To all who have been a part of this journey in even the slightest way, I give thanks and honor your love and support that can make things happen … moving mountains.

Testimonials

"Gail, I look forward to your sharing your empowering questions each day! Thank you for your insights, your light, and your wisdom!"

JANIS HARTLEY, TOP PRODUCING LAKE GENEVA, WI REAL ESTATE AGENT

"Gail, Question 229 – be more aware of the quiet moments, is an excellent question. I may borrow that for my morning meditation... Wow. If it wasn't so late I would have read the whole book. Love 332, this rebirth that is me & 316, acting on the right opportunity and maintain my relationships... I enjoy learning from you. Wise and Wonderful."

MARY PETERSEN, BRAND PARTNER AT NERIUM INTERNATIONAL, LAKE GENEVA, WI

"Glorious Gail." **ROTH HERRLINGER, ADVISOR, BRAINRUSH, LOS ANGELES**

"Great question Gail. Question 254 – all aspects of my life in balance. Yes, balance is key."

CHRIS DEVINCENTIS, VP, MNG BROKER, COACH & TRAINER, KEEFE REAL ESTATE

"Gail is a dynamic and brilliant leader. She has the ability to facilitate her client's growth and guide them in the right direction, so that they can achieve optimum results and achieve their dreams."

LINDA-ANNE KAHN, AUTHOR, LYMPHEDEMA THERAPIST, CLINICAL AROMA-THERAPIST AND PRESIDENT AT BEAUTY KLINIEK AROMATHERAPY DAY SPA

"She has the ability to ask the right questions to guide the conversation, and then zero in on the most critical nuggets of information in a seemingly free-form discussion."

SHAWN BLACKWELL, MPH, PROGRAM DIRECTOR, ALTAMED, CA.

Contents

I AM more than I detect with my senses, one with the universe,
born of the giants, ever expanding my understanding of why I
chose to be here now. — GAIL KRAFT

Introduction

Anything less than living as the universe directs me is not freedom.

The practice of living a conscious life and making choices that align with your core values, congruent with your heart and with ecology (no harm to you or others), requires daily practice; it is a skill. In order for you to manage your thoughts, your words, and your actions, you must first be aware that you are managing two distinct mind activities: your conscious mind, which is the managing director of your Self, and your subconscious, which comprises all of the little thoughts and sub-thoughts that play out all day and all night in your head. This includes the part of your mind you are not even aware of, where beliefs and meta programs direct all your decisions that may or may not follow instructions from your conscious mind.

You are probably aware of your conscious mind, but what about that little voice in your head? Studies show that 60-95% of the decisions you make and the behaviors you exhibit are from your subconscious mind. What do you think? Do you follow any daily patterns or any traditions? Is this conscious or subconscious activity? Do you get up, shower, put coffee on, eat, and brush your teeth by 6:00 AM? Do you even think about what you are doing when you get up or are you thinking about something totally different? Are these conscious or subconscious actions? When you analyze your actions, it becomes clear that your unconscious mind is driving the ship.

If you picked up this book, chances are you are looking for change somewhere in your life or answers to questions posed from the title of the book. How wonderful would it be if you could use your conscious mind as the purposeful director of your thoughts and your subconscious mind as the engine that makes it all happen? How can you tap into the power of your subconscious mind to accomplish what is meaningful in your life?

I have learned that if you do not like the answers you are getting in your life, then you need to ask better questions. Constructing the right questions for you takes practice, and empowering questions are those that bring you your best results. So, what do you really want? Do you see it clearly in your mind, boldly, brightly, and panoramically? Do you know what it feels like to have your boldest dreams come true? Do you know why you want it? Do you believe you can get it? How about that problem that keeps popping up? Wouldn't it be perfect if you could take whatever problem or challenge that you were having and turn it into a question and watch it magically dissolve?

Learning how to tap into the power of your subconscious mind requires clarity of purpose, focus of your conscious mind on positive, results-oriented action, and the deliberate cultivation of positive daily habits.

Empowering questions have some key elements that will drive your energy and shift your thought pattern. They are:

- There is a presupposition that you are already engaged in the action. "What else can I..."

- The action is time-bound to the present, "right here, right now..."

- The question is always in the positive; not one negative word is used.

There are things in your life you cannot control, but you can learn to control how you react and manage through them. By Krafting empowering questions to live by every day, you engage your conscious and subconscious mind in a manner that brings you freedom to live your life to the fullest, ride the waves of turmoil with confidence, and make decisions that align with who you are.

**MONTH
1**

Day 1

What specific actions can I take to connect better with the people I cherish in a way that supports their needs in the most meaningful way today and forever more?

Day 2

What other strategies can I elicit today and every day to navigate in an even healthier, happier, and more secure manner that supports my continued evolution in the most ecological way?

Day 3

What more can I do right now to be ever more aware of each step I take, releasing that which no longer serves me with even greater love, and supporting my goals emotionally, spiritually, physically, and financially?

Day 4

How else can I be even more centered in this body vessel, knowing that I am able to manage my reaction to everything; knowing that I AM?

Day 5

How else can I masterfully navigate through these lessons before me, in a manner that incorporates their learning into my very fiber with ease and grace right now?

Day 6

What more can I do right now to release, allowing myself to live consciously and courageously, to live with love and compassion, and to live with purpose, emerging simply to be present in this moment?

DAY 7

What more can I do to remain more connected to the universe, knowing that everything I need is within me and in my life right now?

DAY 8

How else can I continue to live with childlike love and curiosity and embrace the lessons and gifts that unfold in front of me each day?

DAY 9

How else can I express the joy I feel each day loving my life, loving myself, and loving my intentions; declaring how blessed I am to be here, present and celebrating life?

Day 10

Who else do I know that can support me in becoming a greater master of tapping into the energy surrounding me and allowing the power and strength to pass through me, clearing my mind, energizing my body, and lifting my soul right now?

Day 11

What else can I do to be even more in alignment with my highest purpose, my deepest love, and my ability to reflect back the best there is in me to others?

Day 12

What more can I do to express how thankful I am for continually becoming braver, warmer, more forgiving, and completely authentic each and every day?

DAY 13

Ask and you will receive! Thank you! Today I honor the space I am in and ask how else can I become even more powerful, crystal clear, and laser focused?

DAY 14

What more can I do to celebrate another glorious day that focuses on fundamentals, family, and fun?

DAY 15

What more can I do to continue to honor who I am and to remain on target with my values and my mission with ease and grace right now?

Day 16

I now know that challenges flow through me, and as I gather the lessons and the gifts, I reach a higher level of awareness. What more can I do to become more elevated and connected to the universe right now and for forever?

Day 17

What else can I do to celebrate the wonders I experience when I bear witness to life shifting, as I release to knowing who I am?

Day 18

What additional resources are available to me right now that ease my navigation through the challenges set before me, knowing these are specifically here to hone, focus, and increase my emotional and spiritual growth?

DAY 19

How else can I attune my awareness so I am even better at understanding the infinite possibilities presented to me each day and how can I best leverage these choices to maximize results today and every day forward?

DAY 20

What more can I do today to embrace the infinite wonders around me and incorporate these into my life?

DAY 21

What else can I do right now to be absolutely unstoppable in achieving my heart's desires?

DAY 22

What else can I do right now to embrace and embody this freedom of boundlessly living to my highest potential?

DAY 23

How else can I delight in my life and snuggle into this warm feeling of love and gratitude, each and every day?

DAY 24

How else can I express how thankful I am in my ever knowing and growing into this being, this I AM?

I AM blessed to welcome the morning light

I AM even more perfect every day with all that I create

I AM abundantly aware of the wonders of Mother Nature

I AM even more connected to my power each and every day

I AM enormously thankful for the infinite opportunities around me and thrilled at my ability to act on just the right one, at just the right moment

I AM even more calm, coherent, creative, and communicative every moment of every day

DAY 25

What more can I do in order to continue moving forward in my evolution, in my power, and in my successful execution of bringing and sharing my gifts to this world?

DAY 26

What more specifically can I do today and every day to navigate in a healthy, happy, and secure manner that serves me and all I encounter?

DAY 27

My health is most important to me and I honor this body temple with every breath I take. I embrace finding more and more avenues of receiving abundance, enhancing my life, expanding my business, and elevating people's experiences. What else can I do to continually seek out healthy surroundings that support my continued increase of abundance today and for forever?

DAY 28

Who do I know right now—personally, spiritually, financially, and romantically—that supports my expanding community of like-minded and valued people?

DAY 29

What more can I do right now to be even more connected with exactly the right contacts to enhance my skill set, accelerate my business, and guide my ever-increasing ability to bring in financial abundance now and forever?

DAY 30

Who in my community right now is aligned with developing more ways to have even greater clarity with healthy choices and move toward living a healthier life each and every day, getting better and better?

DAY 31

I am so very grateful for each and every treasured day. How else can I sharpen my awareness and become ever more focused and open to the infinite opportunities that align with my life's purpose today and every day forward?

MONTH
2

DAY 32

What other strategies can I call on that will solidify my relationships that is totally cognizant of the needs of all? How else can I serve those that are uncomfortable with change and help them experience the best service they can, be open to receive advice, and embrace building a trusting relationship with me today and for forever?

DAY 33

How else can I express my gratitude for all the bounty I receive each and every day?

DAY 34

What more can I do to keep moving forward in my life's work while remaining secure in the here and now?

DAY 35

Where else do I find the strength and wisdom to increase my potentiality—personally, professionally, and financially?

DAY 36

How can I be even more open in such a way that when inspiration comes to me I am further able to let it flow, in a natural and integrated action, with ease and grace?

DAY 37

What more can I do to fully express my awe at the wonders I encounter in the most eloquent manner possible from now until forever?

DAY 38

What else can I do each and every day to be ever more aligned and in tune with the moment, being energized, alert, and refreshed?

DAY 39

I am thankful for being aware of the opportunities available that enhance bringing forth my gifts. How else can I complete my project with ease and grace, right now, and produce precisely what my heart is wishing to manifest?

DAY 40

What more can I be doing right now to build my creations smoothly, timely, and with ease while supporting the process physically, financially, emotionally, and spiritually?

DAY 41

I am more aware, clear, and focused each and every day and so grateful for how this allows creativity to flow in, as, and through me. What more can I do right now to be even more strategic, more effective, and more productive?

DAY 42

How specifically can I better tune in to my intuition and do everything with the intention of supporting those I connect with and know exactly what they need right now?

DAY 43

How can I express myself even more fully, allowing the universe that is me to shine through, in everything I do right now?

DAY 44

What more can I do to be intentionally more open, vulnerable, and loving?

DAY 45

Today I am grateful that I am more and more aware of the miracles around me. With this heightened awareness, how else can I honor and acknowledge my daily awakening to the wonders to be witnessed?

DAY 46

Today I give myself a huge hug and celebrate this remarkable life. How else can I enhance my belief and faith in the guidance of my inner wisdom?

DAY 47

Today I AM! What more can I do each and every day to be even more grounded, in the moment, and know that everything is as it should be?

DAY 48

I embrace being even more curious about what shows up every day and ask, "How does this better serve me and align with my intentions right now?"

DAY 49

What else can I do today to be even quieter and just listen?

DAY 50

Today I am so grateful and I acknowledge that I become even more aware that my love, beliefs, and actions reflect my deepest purpose in life. How else can I become the best of who I am?

DAY 51

I LOVE my life with all my heart. How else can I be even more open, allowing my deepest love and my wildest dreams to be present and show up?

DAY 52

Today, I reflect on my remarkable life. What more can I do to express the meaning and cadence of the language I use and select my words precisely so I elevate each conversation in order to achieve the highest outcome?

Day 53

How can I be more aware of the deep and cleansing breaths I take and listen more closely to how every part of me changes for the better?

Day 54

How else can I be an even better friend, knowing my purpose in this role is to love, openly, without judgment, and hold space for others to unfold?

Day 55

What more can I do right now to be even more purposeful with my forgiveness, so this occurs as a natural action, immediately and fully?

DAY 56

How else can I express that I am so very grateful for the awareness unfolding in my life? I am thankful that each day my perception and perspective becomes clearer, and my intention even more focused, and I am relentless in the belief that I am where I need to be right now.

DAY 57

How can I be even more curious and better understand the gifts I receive each moment of every day?

DAY 58

What else can I do to be more connected, with my heart knowing that this is a day of miracles?

Day 59

Every moment is a precious gift that I am more and more thankful for. What more can I do today to rejoice in the celebration of life?

MONTH
3

DAY 60

What more can I do right now to let the people that have shared time with me know that they are forever precious and loved?

DAY 61

I arise and am thankful for the smile permanently on my face and I know I am blessed to be here. How else can I embrace my awakening as I reacquaint myself with who I AM?

DAY 62

What else can I do right now to be even more focused on completing specifically what I have started so I am fully available for the next chapter?

DAY 63

What more can I do right now to better release and let go of expectations, embrace uncertainty, and allow infinite opportunities that are ecological with me and align with my values into my life with ease and grace always?

DAY 64

I love my life and love who I AM! How do I tap into even more wisdom that enables me to connect more freely with my intuitive knowledge, allowing me to choose that which is in harmony and with grace right now?

DAY 65

What more can I do to set the highest intentions and make time to reflect for the best possible outcome leading to even more abundance, helping me achieve my purpose right now?

DAY 66

How else can I gain even more wisdom in knowing which path is right for me at this very moment with the ability to act on it right now?

DAY 67

I know I make a difference each moment of every day. I continue to evolve as I recognize every challenge has a gift and a lesson in it for me. I embrace my continued evolution and I smile knowing I make a difference now. How else can I continue to look up and embrace my continuous emergence, exponential change, and ever-evolving life in this very precious moment that is now?

DAY 68

Patience is one of life's ever-present lessons and I embrace it as a part of my life. How else can I integrate patience into my life for greater good and prosperity right now?

DAY 69

How else can I incorporate empowering questions into my life right now, knowing that when I ask the right question, the universe unfolds in front of me?

DAY 70

What more can I do to embrace elevating my skills in a way that leverages my gifts and provides a model of leadership that aligns with my core values right now?

DAY 71

Who else do I connect with right now that will show me the right doors that will support my gifts, enhance my life, and improve the universe now and for forever?

DAY 72

I love my life and I am curious about how else can I recommit to my growth, achievement, and wellbeing?

DAY 73

What more can I do today to tap into the love I feel and use it to support my day, to drive my purpose, and to affect relationships in the most meaningful and productive way that assures the highest outcome for all?

DAY 74

Yes, please, more of this as I am so grateful for being surrounded by people who believe in me, people who support me, and people who inspire me. What can I do right now to honor these relationships with even more love and gratitude?

75

What more can I do right now to celebrate how very thankful I am for the blessings I receive? How else can I demonstrate that I become even more in love with the world with every breath I take?

DAY 76

How else can I celebrate and honor my capacity to grow, to connect, and to impact others I touch? What more can I do to show gratitude for this miracle that is me?

DAY 77

How else do I dig even deeper for compassion, caring, and love right now and for forever?

DAY 78

What more can I do today and every day to be even more open, clear, and free, where I am absolutely the purest and the best me ever?

DAY 79

Specifically, what more can I do right now to keep my body in ultimate health?

DAY 80

What more can I do right here and right now to strengthen my confidence? How else can I embrace my unquestioning belief in the core truth, value, and trustworthiness of my every intuition now and for forever?

DAY 81

How else can I show my deepest gratitude right now for all the love and support that has been, is, and will be in my life?

DAY 82

I am ready, willing, and all in for today. The only reality is this very moment, so grab it! What more can I do right now to achieve even more with each step and remain even stronger by operating from a place of clarity and love?

DAY 83

How else can I express gratitude and acknowledge all I have accomplished? What more can I do today to embrace the knowing that I AM right where I need to be just at the right time? And it's good to know that, isn't it?

Day 84

Who else do I know that can help guide me wherever I may be to the perfect community that aligns with my spirit and my vision?

Day 85

What more can I do to enhance my knowing that my talents are greater than I could imagine? How else can I use my gifts in a way that elevates the universe even more, while providing an environment of abundance where my loved ones and I continue to thrive?

Day 86

Where there is pain and sadness, there are lessons in love, forgiveness, and caring. What more can I do today to step fully into gratitude for this life I've been given with the knowledge that I take great care of it on all levels?

DAY 87

How else can I better support this gathering of connected souls who create my community, who inspire each other from a place of love and enlightenment? What more can I do to honor this group and be a part of nourishing each member's growth and dreams? What else can I do to shine light on each member's value and be part of enhancing the gifts they bring to this world?

DAY 88

Today I am motivated to do even more. How else can I enhance my focus on the most important tasks that bring me the perfect results and align my soul with the universe?

DAY 89

Who else can I share my loving, life, and laugher with who also embrace opportunities to learn more, to love more, and to forgive more, and who are on the path to grow financially, spiritually, emotionally, and physically?

DAY 90

What more can I do now to completely embrace the witnessing of change, as I move from inspiration to motivation to activation of my deepest desire?

**MONTH
4**

DAY 91

What else can I do in order to fully exercise my ability to consciously change my life, to believe in me, and to know this is achievable at this very moment?

DAY 92

What more can I do from this moment forward to remain always open and receptive to the brilliance the universe pours through me, as I continue this journey of actualization and participation in raising awareness wherever I go?

DAY 93

How else can I embrace the beauty I create in this world in such a way that it shines light into the dark?

DAY 94

How else can I be even more in tune with embracing the shift in focus on the absolute essentials in my life and celebrate the freedom of space this brings me?

DAY 95

What more can I do right now to express how thankful I am that my past beliefs and behaviors protected me and saved my life at times, while today I continue to live a life where I am present and open to be precisely where I am at this moment?

DAY 96

What more can I do to be clear about the decisions I make and the path I take that completely supports propelling me upward, forward, and through more than I could ever imagine right now?

DAY 97

How else can I express my gratitude as today I just let it happen and sink into the arms of success?

DAY 98

How else can I expand my love of life and continue to nurture this intention every day?

DAY 99

What more can I do to continually hold on to my love that is healing, lifting, and enlightening, lifting my awareness and thankfulness for this amazing gift I share with the world?

DAY 100

What else can I do to demonstrate great care for friends, family, associates, and myself today and to know that this is all I need in my world?

DAY 101

As I hone my skills, there is something greater, more challenging, and serves more purpose right here for me to embrace. How else can I be even stronger in being the creator of my journey and realize that each goal is just a pebble on the path?

DAY 102

What more can I do today to listen and allow those thoughts that serve me to nurture and grow right now and for forever?

DAY 103

How else can I be even more aware of where my energy comes from and where it goes and fully manifest the power in and through me to affect my purpose and my outcome?

DAY 104

How else can I express my gratitude for how I am touched by those I encounter? I take the time to see their light and their love and I witness miracles in return.

DAY 105

What more can I do to express my deepest gratitude for this gift to connect and to love? I fully embrace this family, this Tribe, this world of mine, and I am thankful that I experience miracles every moment.

DAY 106

How else can I experience even more bravery in my continued journey of learning, teaching, growing, and nurturing?

DAY 107

What more can I do right now to increase my awareness of the infinite opportunities available to me in a way that I surround myself even more with the powers and skills I need to continue my evolution and transformation in bringing everyone I touch to an even higher vibration right now?

DAY 108

How else can I recognize and celebrate the miracles of life with each breath at each moment as I feel the sun, feel the breeze, and smell the air?

DAY 109

What do I do today to be even more aligned with Divine Timing (the Law of Gestation) and be even more adept at this metamorphosis I call life?

DAY 110

Knowing that this is a brand-new moment and that I evolve anew with every breath I take, how else can I be crystal clear about my choices in this moment of light and what more can I do to embrace the gifts I bring with purpose?

DAY 111

How else may I capture each opportunity presented to me that allows me to be creative and to bring out the best in who I am and what I have to offer?

DAY 112

What more can I do to express my gratitude for the lightness in my heart and shine the light that brings perspective to everything I encounter?

DAY 113

I am so grateful for embracing this gift of childlike curiosity about this journey I am on, How else do I nurture this deep, warm passion even more?

DAY 114

How else can I be open and available for family and friends and have more freedom to embrace their love and to play?

Day 115

How else can I even more fully embrace with ease and grace the achievement of bringing my passion to this world while continually enhancing my quality of life right now and for forever?

Day 116

What more can I do to be even more steadfast in my knowing and, like the power of a mustard seed, move mountains?

Day 117

Who else do I know who can help me be even more aware of the thoughts and words I harness every moment in order to continue living at the purest and highest vibration that is focused on my life's purpose and that is in harmony with the universe?

Day 118

How can I attract even more amazing people in my life right now that I may model, that will support my achieving greater excellence in my work and in my life, and that will affect me in a way that continues to be of benefit to those I am committed to serve?

Day 119

What else can I do right now to honor and tend my finances and engage in revenue-generating activities that are in alignment with my greater purpose and sustain my highest vibration?

Day 120

What else specifically can I do when I experience a reaction to a trigger and how else may I embrace being curious? Where is there more opportunity to grow, to learn, and to shift my perspective?

MONTH
5

DAY 121

How else can I continue to make the perfect choice each moment of every day that honors my mind, body, and spirit in a way that brings me optimal health, wealth, and happiness?

DAY 122

What other ways may I incorporate clearing, cleansing, and enlightening meditation into my daily practices right now that aligns with my life's purpose?

DAY 123

How else may I quiet my mind and listen more closely to my intuitive wisdom every moment of every day, knowing that therein lies the perfect answers for me right now?

Day 124

How else may I ask even greater empowering questions in every aspect of my life that allow me to fully embody the highest and purest that I can possibly be and that support my evolutions and those of the people I touch?

Day 125

What more can I do right now to embrace how the questions I ask impact my life with their energy and become even more empowering with each and every breath I take?

Day 126

What more can I do to express my gratitude knowing that I am in exactly the right place, doing exactly the right thing, and manifesting a life that is exactly as it should be? And it's good to know that, isn't it?

DAY 127

How else may I expand my love and grace in such a way as to provide even more specific space for healing and tap into more compassion easily in order to recognize how beautiful every soul I encounter is?

DAY 128

Knowing that this is a brand-new moment, how else can I live tapping into a greater expanded awareness, which allows my perception to grow more brightly and more vividly with every brand-new moment?

DAY 129

What more can I do in this and every moment to bring all my resources into the now and be totally with my purpose while embracing health, energy, and balance throughout my mind, body, and soul?

DAY 130

What else can I do to consciously and subconsciously be even more in alignment with absolutely believing in who I am and why I am here while every decision and every act's purpose is in that direction?

DAY 131

What more can I do to express my deepest gratitude for the gift of more thoroughly understanding my life with every breath I take?

DAY 132

How can I embrace even more loving my life and celebrate my experiences that allow me to step into my power, my inspiration, and my journey?

DAY 133

What more can I do in this and every moment to become completely one, in peace, with my spirit, with my core, with my soul?

DAY 134

How else can I sink into the vast space allotted to me in the silence that is presented? What is the gift? What is the lesson? What more can I do to settle into this space called peace right now and for forever?

DAY 135

Knowing that every individual comes from their own space of understanding, how else can I shine light on each situation in a manner that illuminates and provides Divine guidance?

DAY 136

How can I support all those I touch, surrounding them in my thoughts, while holding space for them to get through this moment knowing they are loved?

DAY 137

With utmost gratitude I honor my intuitive power and ability to know exactly what I need at precisely the right moment. How else can I hone this skill to remain even more connected with the knowledge of what is perfect for this very moment?

DAY 138

How else can I become even more aware of the unique choices available that resonate with my life's purpose in a way that elevates the universe and provides the resources I need to be unstoppable moving forward? What more can I do right now to embrace the miracle that is me courageously acting, without question?

DAY 139

What more can I do to be even more fully present with my time, my focus, and my soul? How else can I do whatever it takes to be fully here, right now, and completely in this moment and know that this is exactly where I am supposed to be, doing exactly what I am supposed to do?

DAY 140

How else can I demonstrate that I AM centered and focused in such a way that I am a magnet, pulling in everything I need into my space of here and now, today and forever?

DAY 141

What more can I do to embrace the magic that happens when I connect, surrender, and breathe into this existence, surrendering to the miracle of love?

DAY 142

With deepest gratitude I ask, how else I can honor the souls that have come into my life as they mirror the depths of my being and the vastness of the universe?

DAY 143

How else can I be even more completely present while embracing moments of learning, organizing, and prioritizing in order to be totally aware of exactly what serves me and those I serve, and elevates this world to the next level?

DAY 144

What more can I do to fully express my gratitude for the creative ideas that continue to flow more freely every day in support of ways I can more genuinely express myself through my work, through my creativity, and through my language?

DAY 145

How else can I daily increase my clarity in a manner that is transparent and allows energy to flow in, of, and through me, knowing that every moment is a miracle and is real?

DAY 146

What more can I do right now to listen even more to the lessons presented to me each moment and recognize the gift that is mine?

DAY 147

What more can I do right now and forever to be even more specific with exactly what I need precisely when that is in alignment with the greater good? How else can I elicit congruency with my requests, needs, and expectations in a manner that is achievable by all?

DAY 148

How else can I fully embrace this inspiration right now that reveals the truth of supreme manifestation?

DAY 149

What more can I do each moment of every day to expand my capacity of aligning with the universe in love and happiness; knowing that this is who I AM?

DAY 150

How else can I express my eternal gratitude to my friends, family, and Tribe who share their hearts openly and purely so I may see who they are and grow even more in their presence?

DAY 151

What more can I do in this very moment to uncover and share the perfect wisdom needed that elevates my space to the highest vibration of love?

MONTH
6

DAY 152

What more can I do now and for forever to be even more aware of the absolute pure energy surrounding me, the universe, and beyond in such a way that I align perfectly with this ultimate vibration?

DAY 153

How else can I better understand and align with the concept of reality? If everything I believe to be real is a reflection of my beliefs, is it real or my reflection of a desired truth when I connect to the highest of vibration and align with all source of energy? Does it really matter what is real or does the energy from real thought patterns bring into existence the real truth? The answer is the question.

DAY 154

What more can I do from now until forever to be sure the blessings I receive and transmute into my gifts are manifested in exactly the right time and in exactly the right way and benefit exactly the right souls?

DAY 155

What more can I do right now and for forever to embrace this Tribe I am connected to in spirit and live in their light-filled, sacred circle of love and friendship?

DAY 156

I am so very thankful for what has manifested in my life and am curious: what more can I do right now to continue moving forward, expanding my circle of influence, in order to positively impact more and more people every day in an empowering way?

DAY 157

How else can I be even more aware of exactly what people in my life need in this very moment in order to release their fear and elevate their life?

DAY 158

Today I declare that I love this life! What more can I do right now to become even more connected and more aware of the miracle of conscious existence and how this energy, this source, this God power flows in, as, and through us all?

DAY 159

What more can I do each and every day to embrace powerful moments of reflection, meditation, and creative thinking that allows the power to think, reflect, offer up thanksgiving, and pray?

DAY 160

How else can I broaden my perception and look at life's abundance while being in awe as I see how I have been held, nourished, and guided on this perfect path for me?

DAY 161

How else can I enhance my intention to follow my purpose while I express my love and gratitude for this catalyst that propels me forward in faith and confidence?

DAY 162

With love and gratitude, I reflect on my declarations and feel the love this universe has for me and how words, thoughts, and prayers propel me even more to greater levels of awareness and trust. It's good to know that, isn't it?

DAY 163

How else can I continuously focus on moving my energy forward and embrace the knowing that there is everything to be achieved in every moment?

DAY 164

What more can I do right now to elevate my experience on this journey of learning, sharing, and giving in new and powerful ways?

DAY 165

How can I be even more aware of the emotions of others, where they are coming from, and how I show up in support.

DAY 166

I AM open to greatness beyond what I could ever imagine. How else can I be even more open to trusting this time, this day, this very hour as being mine and allow my light to shine through with greater ease?

DAY 167

What specifically must I do today and every day to gather the gifts and lessons from every circumstance and know that this is perfect?

DAY 168

Today I wrap my arms around life and celebrate that I AM! What more can I do to express my joy and embrace moments of relaxing into my life right now?

DAY 169

What other specific action can I take right now that is in complete alignment with my purpose, that has a positive impact on others, and that remains in tune with the positive vibrations of the universe?

DAY 170

The bird chirping resonates in my mind, the cat breathing moves with my rhythm, and the breeze creates music for my ears. I am listening. How can I be even more aware that I come from a center so deep and so calm that there is beauty in the silence?

DAY 171

What else can I do to be clearer, knowing there is more than I ever could dream of here with me right now? I'm wondering who else can feel it, too. Embrace it, sink into it, and believe it.

DAY 172

How else can I sink into the joy of letting go, allowing what is meant to be happen, with total trust?

DAY 173

What more can I do to explore this discovery of the peace within me that keeps me centered while the purpose I bring to my work and to my relationships becomes more powerful?

DAY 174

I am curious, how else can I embrace this reality that I am both vulnerable and protected and that I love who I AM every moment of every day from now until forever?

DAY 175

How do I continue bravely remaining centered and connected now and forever so I am in my empowered state, coming from love?

DAY 176

How else can I remember every moment to stay focused on being right here, right now, allowing tomorrow to unfold as it will, knowing that all will turn out as is intended?

DAY 177

How else do I expand my Tribe and collaborate with those who follow their passion, knowing that it's time to take action?

DAY 178

What more can I do to extend my sphere of influence and connect with those that have been waiting for my gift, knowing that it is time?

DAY 179

What more can I do to express that I AM present, I AM wrapped in hugs, I emanate peace, I AM a provider, I radiate love, I manifest abundance, and I shine the light?

DAY 180

How else can I expand my awareness and listen more closely to my body's whispers, trust more openly in my intuitive wisdom, and be even more confident in my actions?

DAY 181

How else can I daily speak in a manner that aligns with health, happiness, and prosperity while supporting and honoring the success of others as I would my own?

MONTH
7

DAY 182

What more can I do each and every day to connect with family, friends and co-workers, letting them know that each and every one of them is special?

DAY 183

How can I be better able to present and share my gifts in the most appropriate way that honors my intention, is in alignment authentically with my values, and raises the vibration of those I touch now and for forever.

DAY 184

What more can I do today and every day to assure my words and my thoughts are precise and wisely chosen, allowing me to be even more focused on working for the highest outcome?

DAY 185

How else can I thank the universe for giving me absolutely everything I ask for and reinforce my daily intention to be strong and steadfast in goals and my peace of mind?

DAY 186

What more can I do each and every day to bring even greater awareness to those I touch that we are all connected, that everything is within each one of us, and that we are a reflection of love?

DAY 187

How else do I clearly express my thankfulness and my love of who I AM openly and lovingly as I continue to grow and show up and am absolutely present and bring value to this life in each moment?

DAY 188

How else can I be even more clear, targeted, and specific with the choices I make with my language so I speak from love and my words are received with open hearts?

DAY 189

How else can I continually nurture and illuminate exactly the right opportunities for those I encounter while continuing massive growth and security with love?

DAY 190

How else can I celebrate my life and bravely embrace this metamorphosis as I change with every breath I take and, with every moment of time, I am constantly transforming?

DAY 191

How can I be even better at listening in order to more clearly hear the answers to "what is the gift" or better understand when to "let it go" and always to remember to "breathe," giving space that lets in solutions?

DAY 192

What more can I do to relax and give in to my learning, specifically the learning that is in the giving?

DAY 193

Knowing that I am focused and caring and that my purpose is to clear a path for those that I touch, then I wonder, how else can I become even more consistent today and every day forward, remaining detached from fear and anchored in love?

DAY 194

What more can I do to embrace each moment, allowing whatever is coming to me to flow in while becoming even more relaxed into the now?

DAY 195

Having experienced balance and being centered in the moment, how else can I learn to continuously let energy flow through while remaining unmoved and know that I AM connected and aware of infinite possibilities?

DAY 196

Knowing that I continue to evolve and live at a different vibration, I wonder, what more can I do to love those moving up the ladder behind me with compassion and the understanding that they are each on a path that is different than mine and is theirs alone to travel?

DAY 197

When energy is erupting and throwing me off balance, what more can I do at this very moment to see the lesson, embrace the gift, and let it be?

DAY 198

How else do I recognize, embrace, and act on that which is presented to me as the highest means to translate my success ecologically, financially, and spiritually this moment and forever?

DAY 199

Knowing that true reality is love, tenderness, and caring; how else can I embrace knowing that the truth will set me free?

DAY 200

How else can I embrace being even more certain that the reality of pure happiness and beauty is true, now and forever?

DAY 201

What more can I do each and every day to help those drawn to me to better understand how to act, relate, and communicate differently to achieve their dreams?

DAY 202

How else am I able to facilitate accelerating internal change in a way that is in alignment with those I work with and elevates the universe for the greater good?

DAY 203

I embrace knowing the change of the lunar cycle and wonder how else I can enjoy the pull of the sister planet circling what once was her home?

DAY 204

I love Divine influence, knowing that everything has its time and unfolds as it should. What more can I do to remain connected to the Law of Gestation and allow the evolution of my growth to emerge?

DAY 205

How else can I celebrate living right here and right now, knowing that this is a brand-new moment?

DAY 206

What more can I do to remain quiet and allow other doors to open as I wait just one more moment and listen?

DAY 207

Who else can I bring into my circle of mutual support and growth where we become even more consistent in being present, honoring our gifts and our lives?

DAY 208

What can I do this day to see even further beyond the obvious and into the essence of life itself, knowing that what I thought was real was that which I believed to be true?

DAY 209

How am I able to take even more responsibility for my feelings, my decisions, and my results? What more can I do to take time right now to be present and look within to understand the depths of who I AM now, tomorrow, and forever?

DAY 210

What more can I do right now to be even more diligent in nurturing my love and celebrating with joy each moment of this life? It is through this celebration my energy flows into my relationships and I am in awe of the people I can touch.

DAY 211

With a clear lens, expanded awareness, and deep-seeded love, I see the world vibrating and inviting me in, allowing me to tap in and partake, to check in, to be present, and to be a participant. I listen and hear the subtle messages and follow their lead with trust, with love, and with intention. After all, am I not just leading myself? Who better to follow and who better to trust now and for forever?

DAY 212

I realize that in my listening I hear more than words and in my speaking I barely communicate the depths of what I am sharing. In my very touch I move others; in my very look I see deep within their souls; in my vulnerability I them you the real me. How else can I show others how truly they are loved?

MONTH
8

DAY 213

I now know that the heart love I have come to know is eternal, all-encompassing, and powerful and that the energy from this knowing is transformative. How else can I embrace today's transformation knowing that this process breaks me through to the other side of greatness?

DAY 214

What can I do right now to better examine this feeling and take a closer look at the root, the core, and the source? The closer I get, the better I understand that this energy is either love or fear. What better choices can I make in this very moment, knowing that I AM deeply rooted, that I AM totally open, and that I AM immeasurably strong, in order to continue to anchor me to love forever?

DAY 215

How else can I tap into the specific language and the precise approach that empowers me, others, and the world to always hear the words between the spaces and to continue to select the language that is heard beyond the noise?

DAY 216

How else can I further expand my sphere of influence while honing my skill as the perfect conduit to allow people to become even more aware of their full potential while consistently living their life and mine intentionally?

DAY 217

What more can I do right here and right now to better embrace trusting myself, knowing that I always make exactly the right choices, so I can better step into the knowing that I show up as needed, and to release with abandon into expressing that I AM?

DAY 218

Knowing that growth is eternal, who is the perfect model for me at this moment and forward who is a supreme representation of who I am becoming, spiritually, financially and vocationally, so I may manifest this vision right here, right now, and for forever?

DAY 219

After taking a moment to imagine visions of our universe, I know there is so much more to know. How can I further expand the way that I perceive my world, allowing infinitely more inspiration to naturally flow through me as I surrender into this process?

DAY 220

While standing on the edge of the unknown, what more can I do right now to let go even more and step into the quiet and calm of this moment?

DAY 221

How can I better hold space for those in need at specifically the right moment in exactly the right way, knowing that in the nothingness is everything, and I AM here?

DAY 222

How else can I embrace each emotion I experience, recognizing change, knowing I AM strong, remaining present in each moment, while listening to my inner wisdom?

DAY 223

How else can I transmute my intuitive wisdom to better influence balance, perspective, and collaboration in order to develop even greater leaders?

DAY 224

What more can I do today and every day to dig even deeper while I simultaneously release into the moment and step into what unfolds before me?

DAY 225

How else can I embrace my beloved, honoring this blessed union of love with the light that sustains life now and through eternity?

DAY 226

What more can I do to more fully express the gifts I brought into this world and continue stirring the hearts of others, illuminating the way for all to embrace being human, warts and all?

DAY 227

How else can I express my deepest desire for others in order for them to know my love for them lies deep in my heart forever and that they know love is glorious?

DAY 228

What more can I do now to be even more aware of each breath I take that brings healing light into every cell of my body and each breath I let out that releases me and relaxes me into connecting with this moment?

DAY 229

How can I be even more aware of the quiet moments that are for connecting, refreshing, and rejuvenating while I more fully embrace the moments between the breaths, the space between the lines, and the thoughts between the actions right now?

DAY 230

Knowing that fear is a projection of what might be and probably won't be, what more can I do to put these thoughts behind me and more bravely move forward in the moment, with purpose, focus, and dedication now and forever in every moment?

DAY 231

We all came here to have the human experience, to connect with each other, and to learn. Therefore, what more can I do right now to remember why I chose to be here, to more fully step into my purpose, and to continue supporting the elevation of this planet right here and right now?

DAY 232

How else can I embrace my connection with love—personal love, universal love, wild love, broken love, and whole love—knowing this brings me a deeper understanding and greater passion as I alchemize this experience, elevating my vibration and enhancing that of this planet?

DAY 233

What more can I do right now to continually heal my mind, body, and soul as I remain free of the past and continue living a healthy life that empowers me to continue to soar towards and accomplish my purposes?

DAY 234

How else can I connect with my inner core and be even more aware of my capacity to enjoy nature, remembering that this link is part of staying whole and is directly related to my increasing capacity to heal all relationships in my life?

DAY 235

How else can I further support my open and honest self-knowledge, allowing me to transcend even more into the understanding that I am here to give, to share, and to live as my intuitive wisdom directs me?

DAY 236

In all relationships, what I see is a mirror and what I am is a mirror. How can I better reflect back to others and show them everything that is holding them back, thus waking them up so they can elevate their lives right now?

DAY 237

How else can I nurture my daily growth, knowing it's limitless, while showing up to each day embracing luscious revelations and new discoveries?

DAY 238

What more can I do this moment and every moment from now and to forever to embrace the powerful I AM, boldly stepping into the many purposes and gifts I am born with, knowing that this is exactly as it should be, and it's good to know that, isn't it?

DAY 239

How can I be even more open to elevating my perspective and my energy each and every moment, allowing me to be aware of the people sharing my journey and being sure they are aware of how important they are in my life?

Day 240

Who else do I know that can stand beside me, holding space for the losses I feel, allowing me to work through the energy, uncover the lesson, and hold on to the gift as I walk through to the other side?

Day 241

I've come to understand that Soulmates have come into my life at exactly the right time to reflect back a deeper understanding of who I AM and they leave when my lesson is complete. How else can I embrace these special souls in my life and thank them even more profoundly for their gifts?

Day 242

What more can I do right now to shed disempowering beliefs and be even more aligned with the highest energy of the universe, knowing that I step into an understanding that I AM forever changing, forever growing, and forever manifesting a state of being every moment in the choices I make?

DAY 243

In understanding the laws of manifestation, I know my thoughts and my words create my experience. Knowing this is true, how else can I remain ever more diligent about the direction of my thoughts, honoring that which is in my heart, knowing that what I believe is real and achievable right now?

MONTH
9

DAY 244

What more can I do to tap into my intuition and trust it ever more explicitly while I remain even more connected with life's ebb and flow, the rhythm of nature?

DAY 245

When I am quiet, I feel energy emerging. What more can I do to tap into my strength, empowered and enlightened, and like the flicker of the butterfly wing, move the world?

DAY 246

What more can I do this very moment to step into the change that awaits me, allowing me to fully express my gifts and my talents and to daily elevate my vibration, drawing exactly what and who I need into my life right now?

DAY 247

Universe, I hear you. It's time to remove the blinders I've had on that I named "focus" and to be even more open to what you have in store for me. What more can I do right here and right now to move forward with what has been placed before me in order to better share my impact on more and more people every day in a positive, empowering way?

DAY 248

How can I be even more aware and recognize, embrace, and act with the highest intention of what I am driven to do in this world while transforming my success ecologically, spiritually, and economically now and for forever?

DAY 249

What more can I do every moment to honor this life and give thanks that I have connected with what makes my heart dance while I live my life to the fullest and know that I AM alive?

DAY 250

There are the subtle gifts, these small surprises that show up to support me every day, that let me know this is right and this is good. How else can I demonstrate my deepest gratitude for what life has given me today and for forever?

DAY 251

How can I be even more brave with my intuitive wisdom and channel this energy for the greatest good possible, knowing that every day I plant yet another seed of wisdom.

DAY 252

I've noticed that every moment is full of adventure and presents an opportunity to grow. What more can I do to enhance this experience, expand this knowledge, and explore what might be?

DAY 253

Knowing that I show up when others are ready for me, I gain a new respect for how I am a tool, a vehicle that contributes to this world. Knowing this allows me to be even more curious and so I wonder, how else can I better assure that all aspects of my life are honored and in balance mentally, emotionally, spiritually, physically, and financially while I continue to keep all energy in alignment?

DAY 254

What more can I do right now to settle into my being, breathe deeply, and be even more patient in taking the time for deeper curiosity and understanding of truth?

DAY 255

While taking the time to love family and friends, I examine how we are together and yet apart. Knowing this I wonder, what more can I do to hold space to see each person's beautiful spirit shine through and to thank them for being part of my life?

DAY 256

How can I be even more open and aware of exactly the perfect opportunity that is in front of me right now, while knowing that this is exactly what I need, that this specifically uses my skills and capabilities, and that this elevates the universe when I step into this life today?

DAY 257

What more can I do in this very moment to give into the chaos that is constantly with me as I more fully embrace my transformation and its creation?

DAY 258

How can I be even better right now at celebrating me, complimenting that I AM, and encouraging my exploration into the unknown?

Day 259

How else can I better look at life to become even more of the observer, looking through all eyes, and better understand what is?

Day 260

Now that I have begun this journey, how else can I better connect with this soul that has chosen to manifest in this body and allow the vibration of the universe peek through?

Day 261

What other resources can I tap into that keep me even more focused on my purpose with even more joy, more love, and more laughter right now?

DAY 262

What more can I do right now to crystalize my purpose and better align with the universal intelligence that is forever flowing through me?

DAY 263

How can I be even more skilled at doing better than my very best each and every moment of every day?

DAY 264

How can I better express how I see each soul, how I know each one, and how I love them all and vow that I will show up, be present, and feel fully even more with complete abandonment right now and for forever?

DAY 265

What more can I do right now to demonstrate how thankful I am that I laugh, cry, hurt, heal, fall, rise, play, work, live, and die as the person I am meant to be, connected in universal love, knowing that this is as it should be? And it's good to know that, isn't it?

DAY 266

How else can I be even more consistent in doing exactly what I love to do, precisely what I was meant to do, and even more fully embrace the miracle of abundance this brings into my life right now and for forever?

DAY 267

What more can I do today to step into more completely allowing all those I love to be exactly what they have chosen to be, following their path and living their destiny?

Day 268

What can I do right now to continue letting go even more, observing the game as I find myself laughing out loud, living life with passion, and just loving the ride?

Day 269

What more can I do at this very moment to give extreme thanks and acknowledge that my gifts, my capabilities, and my passion all come together in Divine time? And I know this is good, isn't it?

Day 270

What else can I do right now to be even more graceful moving through each day with love and with ease, knowing that I am in continuous alignment with the universe now and for forever?

DAY 271

How can I be even more curious each and every day about how naturally I connect with both Mother Earth and Father-Mother-God-Source simultaneously and in harmony, expanding my understanding of the One?

DAY 272

Knowing that this is a brand-new moment, what can I do to even more effortlessly transform my thoughts and my language in way to bring in even more love and abundance while I remain rooted in the constant flow and connection of the universe?

DAY 273

How else can I release into the trust of the process even more while being even more confident of who I AM right now?

DAY 274

What more can we do right now to help our world better understand that we are all connected and what happens to one actually happens to us all and that it is through each individually opening up his and her awareness every moment of every day that we begin to truly see each other?

MONTH
10

DAY 275

How can I be even more connected to my amazing community in such a way that I show my deepest appreciation and gratitude today and forever for the gifts that have been given to me by the miracle of angels that have touched my life?

DAY 276

What more can I do each and every day to be even more aware of the universe I am connected to, that from which all things manifest, and tap deeply into truth?

DAY 277

How else can I align and harmonize between the physical, mental, and spiritual realms and better know myself, thus gain a deeper understanding of the mysteries of the Universe?

Day 278

What can I do right now to elevate my vibration even more through my five physical senses as well as my mental and intuitive mind, assuring the purest of energy continues to be created?

Day 279

What more can I do each and every moment to be even more masterful at understanding and managing the duality of nature, thus transforming my thoughts by consciously raising my vibration to access the polar opposite of any situation at will immediately?

Day 280

What more can I do right now to better understand and minimize the swaying of my thoughts, knowing that this ebb and flow is a natural action in the universe?

DAY 281

How else can I master my thoughts, words, and actions, knowing that everything in my reality is an effect of my mental creation?

DAY 282

What more can I do right now and forever to better tap into and embrace my expression of both feminine and masculine energy, knowing that these qualities lie within me now and by bringing them together I AM complete?

DAY 283

How can I be more aware of aligning even more purposefully with the Law of Attraction, knowing that this reality is the basis of the laws of the universe?

DAY 284

What more can I do to be even more present with holding space and being cognizant with my thoughts, as the energy of my ideas are like seeds planted and can only manifest into the physical experience by patience, nurturing, and nourishment?

DAY 285

How else can I become even more masterful at managing the reality that is a product of my unconscious, knowing that I attract what I believe in my subconscious mind and that I have the power to change this right now by conscious design?

DAY 286

What more can I do to openly embrace the discomfort of chaos and allow myself to step more bravely into life's spectacular gifts right now?

DAY 287

How else do I improve my daily focus and become even more masterful at being ever more specific in utilizing supreme communication and enhance the quality of my language in this very moment?

DAY 288

How do I become even more open to the realization that this reality is a construct of my thoughts and that the "I" that I am is always at the highest vibration?

DAY 289

What more do I do each moment to listen to what is being spoken and to be ever more skillful at quieting the noise that I sometimes hear?

Day 290

How else do I connect with my intuition to such a degree that every moment of every day I know I am tapped into achieving ultimate results?

Day 291

When thoughts, feelings, or circumstances are not serving me, I get curious. What is the root cause, how can I breathe even more deeply, what gift is there for me to incorporate into my life? The breath directs my mind and my mind directs my thoughts. Breathe!

Day 292

What more can I do to feel the vibration of my thoughts through The Supreme Consciousness and to propel my mind on the Divine path and unfold my complete potentiality and enlightenment?

DAY 293

Each breath I take brings healing light into every cell of my body, and each breath I let out releases me and relaxes me into connecting with this moment. How else can my gifts continue to touch the hearts of those I hold in my life?

DAY 294

How else can I express how thankful I am for all the opportunities before me that I can explore, allowing miracles to happen?

DAY 295

What more can I do right now to share this lesson that we are at the start, the middle, and the end of change and are free-falling? Let's spread our wings to soar!

DAY 296

How do I become even more confident and allow the universe to unfold, knowing that I AM where I am meant to be and that my lessons are miracles, my gifts to this life?

DAY 297

How else can I live each moment with heartfelt awareness of today's beauty, wonder, and magic in such a way that it continues to enhance all my interactions now and for forever?

DAY 298

Who else do I bring into my community now whose energy and purpose supports my further evolution of tapping into the wisdom of utilizing all my resources at exactly the right moment in order to more accurately propel me to participate in elevating the vibration and enhancing the connection of all I encounter?

DAY 299

How else do I embrace these moments of magic when I notice there are no thoughts, feeling boundless and complete in the silence?

DAY 300

Knowing that time is a relative construct, how else do I expertly maximize my activities and better achieve what must be completed now while I continue to keep my personal relationships and commitments as promised?

DAY 301

How else do I fully tap into my intuition, my imagination, and my creativity in this very moment in order to fully experience the strength that is me and know that my goals, my purpose, and my calling make me unstoppable, make me invincible, and make me on target today and every day forward?

DAY 302

How else do I embrace the process of rebuilding, realizing that in this moment the tearing down of my walls results in the reconstruction that has been my purpose all along?

DAY 303

What more can I do right now to expand my ability to be ever more positive in a manner that allows me to be even more fluid, like mercury flowing, endless energy infused into my very being?

DAY 304

What new rituals can I embrace right now in honor of this time of moving inward in perspective and gathering of community?

MONTH
11

DAY 305

How else do I honor my journey of enlightenment as my pace has slowed down, my movement is more deliberate, my reflection is more focused, and my meditation brings more connection?

DAY 306

What more can I do right now to find more time for diving into a good book and settling in with a warm fire while wrapped snuggly in a blanket, joined contently by my cat curled in my lap?

DAY 307

How else do I tap into the daily practice right now that supports my ability to slide even more naturally into activities that are for my continued physical, mental, and spiritual wellbeing and enlightenment?

Day 308

How else do I remain in touch with my deeper self while reflecting pure heart and pure purpose with love?

Day 309

Knowing that the entire cosmos follows the natural laws of the universe, and in this unification there is an energy called God, Source, Creator, or Science, what more can I do to live according to this Divine order and the glorious beauty of creation?

Day 310

While feeling the chill of Winter, I am reminded that the change of the seasons brings an energetic and spiritual shift that is felt more deeply when I am living within the season. How else can I deeply embrace the slowing of winter and celebrate the vibration it brings that allows reflection and introspection?

DAY 311

In the power called Spring, the Sun increases as I begin to feel empowered to reach out for what I want and connect to the Earth again. What more can I do to connect with my potential and potency in this time and create even more opportunities for even greater positive change in my life and the lives of other, birthing actions that come from my heart?

DAY 312

Summer fire, you bring me warmth, movement, growth and relationship. What more can I do in acknowledging this energy right now in order to create even more connection to people, laughter, and light that continues forever?

DAY 313

The letting go of Autumn is the time when nature rids itself of what is not needed, allowing me a chance to look beyond myself and allow connection to the spirit and to others. What more can I do right now and forever to be even more connected to the heavenly realms and gain a deeper understanding that I AM connected to all that is and I AM the source of my true self?

DAY 314

Given that this is a new day, what more can I do to bring my attunements into each moment and remain even more present, more fresh, and more connected with the universe while anchored in Gaia?

DAY 315

In what ways can I greater acknowledge full responsibility here and now for everything I experience, knowing this is a shadow of the past, and respond in a way that results in the positive/beneficial reactions of people around me?

DAY 316

Knowing that there are infinite possibilities and that I have unlimited resources, what more can I do right now to act on exactly the right opportunity for my specific gifts, my financial wealth, and my continued evolution that also holds space for my presence and devotion to my loved ones?

DAY 317

What more can I do now to step, with ease and grace, even further and more fully into my creative power right now and achieve even more with my gifts each and every day?

DAY 318

How can I gather my learnings with even more grace and ease with absolute confidence, presence, and poise knowing that I AM UNSTOPPABLE in increasing my productivity now as I continue to propel my career and my life efficiently and prosperously forward into the future?

DAY 319

If I am but a reflection of the thoughts of others and they are but a reflection of mine, how else can I be even more in tune with others' perceptions and through my evolving awareness, continue to bring out more of my love and understanding into my relationships?

DAY 320

What more can I do today to be even more present, knowing the one truth about the past is that it is not here today?

DAY 321

Knowing that I have the Power to tap into unstoppable energy and to channel whatever I want to manifest, how else can I further use these gifts now and into the future for the greater good, greater energy, and greater abundance?

DAY 322

Knowing that my mind rebuilds my brain with new experiences every moment, how else can I consciously use this awareness to construct even deeper, more enlightened values and beliefs right now?

DAY 323

How else can I embrace the mystery of life, look into its magic, dance with its music, and be even more delighted with this experience of freedom?

DAY 324

How else can I strengthen my knowing right now that I have everything I need to enjoy this present moment and to immediately let go of any expectations based on my past or my imagined future?

DAY 325

How else can I bring my consciousness to my core and pay even more attention to the space between each breath, and listen?

DAY 326

What more can I do right now to better shift what is perceived as a problem into the understanding that this is simply life experienced?

DAY 327

What else can I do today to consistently choose to speak from my core, being ever more still in each moment and knowing that I AM?

DAY 328

What more can I do right now to continue selecting the path of love, knowing that every time I choose to work on my heart's desire—that which resonates with me at the deepest level—I fulfill my purpose and choose joy?

DAY 329

Universal energy is forever changing, transforming; what more can I do right now to harness my power and fine tune my vibration to the perfect pitch, embracing an even more robust life?

DAY 330

What more can I do right now to allow nature's ebb and flow to pass through me, knowing this is but the rhythm of the universe and is part of my connection to others?

DAY 331

How can I be even more masterful in my ability to disassociate, being the observer in my life, realizing that everything I see and react to is a construct of my feelings and beliefs and "just is" a comparison to something else?

DAY 332

As my vibration shifts, I feel my energy move. This is beautiful and painful, glorious and fearful, and I ask; what more can I do right now to embrace this rebirth that is me?

DAY 333

What more can I do to be even more aware of where I am right now in order to better embrace choosing the path that raises my experience of harmony and fulfillment in my life?

DAY 334

How else do I open with abandon and receive with ease and grace even more of that which aligns with who I AM, allowing me to bring in the energy equal to what I have to give?

DAY 335

Today, how else can I, with absolute certainty, choose the path that is perfect for my spiritual, physical, and financial growth, that honors every relationship, and that is ecologically sound?

MONTH
12

DAY 336

What more can I do right now to relax into my life and accept what is mine, releasing the illusion of fear?

DAY 337

How else can I acknowledge the darkness in my life while living in the light, seeking out and embracing what is positive, ever expanding my mastery over my environment, and sinking into the law of correspondence, bringing my inner light out even more?

DAY 338

Each day I consciously practice mindfulness, actively paying attention to the moments in my life. How else can I bring this practice to the forefront of all my moments?

DAY 339

What more can I do right now to know when to let go and accept others for who they are, gain an even deeper connection with my heart, and develop a truer ability to see what is real right now?

DAY 340

Who else in my circle of friends, my champions, is available right now to witness my evolution and celebrate life, knowing it is impossible to fail?

DAY 341

Part of the journey of increased awareness includes knowing that my experience of reality is mine alone; knowing this, how else do I connect with others' experience with ease and grace, allowing real communication and connection to occur right now?

DAY 342

What more can I do to become acutely aware of the moments that change me and redirect me, and in doing so, allow my life to be forever changed?

DAY 343

How else do I expand my ability to be in tune with every breath I take until I am in a state of contemplation, curiosity, and intuition with everything I do?

DAY 344

What more can I do right now to I expand my curiosity and quiet my mind, expanding my awareness that something incredible is waiting to be known?

Day 345

Knowing that I am connected, inseparable from all that is, how else can I better immerse in the ebb and flow of life, becoming one with its waves?

Day 346

One truth I know is that the concept of wrong is a construct of my belief system and with this knowledge comes power. What more can I do right now to become even more focused and driven and release what little is left that might bind me now and for forever?

Day 347

I have become a master alchemist, uniting all the parts that are me, and in the chaos transformation happens. How can I relax even more into the turmoil, confusion, and mud of the moment knowing what's emerging is an even more complete gem that is me?

DAY 348

Knowing that attaining flawlessness is unachievable as perfection is a momentary construct of the mind, I am, therefore, curious how else can I strive for even more progress, heading to an even higher level of excellence?

DAY 349

I see the magic in this world, its beauty, goodness, and hope. What more can I do right now to continue to see the best in people, embracing a lighter perspective of life, while also realizing that we are imperfect beings here to learn from our imperfections?

DAY 350

How else do I express my gratitude and utilize my innate ability of being aware of the symbolism around me every day and remain forever in the light that shines through the darkness?

Day 351

How else do I break free of illusions that captivate and become ever more aware of my indestructible nature, my malleability, and my ability to embody qualities of the Divine?

Day 352

I have experienced great success and I have walked into great disappointment and have, with purpose, lived fully, boldly, and passionately. How else do I learn from life experiences how to get messy, make mistakes, and bravely go where my heart calls me?

Day 353

What more can I do right now to look past distinctions I have in my mind, knowing these to be untrue?

DAY 354

How do I release even more, allowing myself to be drawn with abandonment inward, outward, and toward that which resonates with me completely?

DAY 355

As I realize my perception is based on the constraints of this world I wonder, what more can I do right now to see past this illusion and reconnect with the beginning?

DAY 356

How else do I remain ever more grounded; listening to my body, my heart, my intuition, and expanding my mind with the power of Self-love, appreciation, and gratitude right now and forever?

Day 357

What more can I do right now to embrace this state of connectedness, this me that is eternal and is more than I AM and yet I AM more?

Day 358

What more can I do right now to help even more people see the goodness they were born with and that through compassion, communication, and understanding they make world better?

Day 359

What more can I do right now to better release seeking goals and completely embrace the curious act of seeking truth?

DAY 360

What more can I do to keep trust and faith in the forefront of my mind, and ever expand my capacity to love?

DAY 361

How can I continue to experience this union of connection—spiritually, mentally, and physically—as I burst free each morning anew and begin again?

DAY 362

What more can I do to continue to release past loved and not so loved ones at any point in time, setting them free of our connection knowing that I do, in fact, love them without attachment now and for forever?

Day 363

How else do I become even more skilled in navigating each experience with wisdom and compassion, assuring an ecological outcome for the highest good, knowing that my perception is a construct and always under my control?

Day 364

What more can I do to listen even more closely and curiously to the chaos and the noise in, through, and around me, allowing me to become part of the resonance we call life, connecting to my Self in peace?

Day 365

How else can I be even more aware of those coming into my life who believe they are stronger, superior, or more enlightened than me and see the truth of their fragility, and how else can I show them there is power in being vulnerable and real?

Day 366

Knowing that at some point I will stumble, what more can I do to support those in my life who see this as a weakness in themselves and help them better understand that this is humanity and they are perfect and complete, always?

About the Author

I trust the path I am on and that I am exactly where I am supposed to be. — Gail Kraft

In this book Gail Kraft has collected empowering questions that she had written for her clients, training programs, and herself. Read one each day, find one that resonates for you, use these and learn how to make your own and watch your world magically change before your very eyes. What else can you do to formulate the right question that will unlock your potential right now?

Gail grew up in Dorchester and Mattapan, neighborhoods of Boston, Massachusetts. She is the last of eight children with most of her siblings entering young adulthood when she was born. As virtually an only child Gail grew up as a latchkey kid, alone until midnight most days, hanging out with a gang at the Smith Street Drug Store in Mattapan.

As an adult, Gail began transforming her own life by learning how to speak without her deep accent and transferring her street-smart approach to life to a street-smart approach to business. She is no longer a tough-speaking gang kid living on the streets of Mattapan and is now a business owner who fully understands how the power of words can destroy or build relationships.

Curious about how to be even better at getting results, Gail started a journey, which brought her through many self-help processes that include formal education, numerous business certifications, and many motivational programs with trainers such as **Niurka, Inc.** and **New Peaks**. She is certified in many coaching/ mentoring techniques and incorporates Neuro-Linguistic Programming and quantum linguistics where she uses language and energy to shift her approach and that of her clients for quick and targeted results. Gail has brought her experience, her training, and her passion for life together in this book of empowering questions so you too can find your way to living beyond your dreams.

Learn more about Gail and her work at:

theempoweringprocess.com